IT Risk Management

Introduction to the main concepts and processes of IT Risk Management

Fabrizio Zuccari

"Il Risk Management nell'IT è come una bussola per la navigazione attraverso le tempeste digitali: senza di essa, ci si trova alla deriva nell'oceano dell'incertezza."

"Risk Management in IT is like a compass for navigating through digital storms: without it, you are adrift in the ocean of uncertainty."

Table of contents

Introduction to IT Risk Management

IT Risk Management is essential for protecting digital assets, ensuring operational continuity, complying with regulations, and preserving corporate reputation. In the following pages, we will explore in detail the phases of the IT risk management process and the common methodologies used.

Definition of key concepts

Let's begin by understanding the concept of risk and its management.

IT Risk

IT risk represents the likelihood of experiencing a financial or reputation loss due to cybersecurity threats. These threats can range from security breaches to service interruptions, human errors, or other situations that can negatively impact the IT environment.

E.g.: Take, for instance, a healthcare organization. It might face the IT risk of a data breach if the computer systems are not adequately protected. Imagine the damage such a breach could cause to the reputation and trust of patients.

IT Risk Management:

IT Risk Management is a strategic process that aims to identify, assess, and mitigate risks associated with the use of information technologies in an organization. This process is crucial because it helps protect digital assets, ensure operational continuity, and achieve business objectives.

Importance of Risk Management in IT

IT risk management is not merely an administrative practice but a vital component for the sustainability and prosperity of organizations in the digital era. Its conscious adoption and integration into the corporate culture represent fundamental investments in addressing the increasingly complex challenges of the contemporary IT landscape.

Let's delve deeper into some key concepts that underscore the centrality of this practice:

- **Protection of digital assets**
  Risk management serves as the primary bulwark against an increasingly sophisticated range of threats. Hackers, malware, and, no less importantly, human errors can compromise the security of critical business assets. Risk management acts as the architect of strategic defense, implementing preventive and reactive measures to ensure the integrity and confidentiality of these digital resources.

- **Operational continuity**
  It's not just a matter of security but also operational

resilience. In the face of negative events such as cyberattacks or natural disasters, it's essential for an organization to maintain its operations. Through robust management of IT risks, companies can plan and implement strategies that allow them to withstand turbulence and quickly resume activities, minimizing financial and operational impact.

- **Regulatory compliance**

  Many industries are subject to specific regulations and norms regarding cybersecurity. Risk management becomes how an organization can ensure compliance with these regulatory provisions. Non-compliance not only exposes the company to potential security risks but can also lead to hefty fines and sanctions. Proactive management of IT risks thus becomes a crucial preventive investment to avoid unwanted legal and financial consequences.

- **Reputation management**

  An organization's reputation is an intangible asset of immeasurable value. A security incident or data loss can cause irreparable damage to the public perception of the company. In this context, IT Risk Management emerges as a protective shield, helping to prevent and mitigate potential reputational crises.

Investing in IT risk management becomes a proactive act of protection, preserving not only data security but also public trust and the solidity of the corporate reputation.

Fundamentals of Risk Management

The identification, assessment, and classification of risks are critical phases in the IT risk management process.

These steps enable the organization to better understand threats, assess their severity and priority, and develop strategies to effectively address them, thereby ensuring security and operational continuity.

Identification of risks in IT

Risk identification is the first step in IT risk management. This process involves recognizing and documenting all potential risks that can threaten the IT environment of an organization. To conduct proper risk identification, a systematic approach involving various methodologies and tools is necessary.

Here are some of the most common techniques used:

- **Brainstorming**:
  Assemble a team of experts, including IT professionals, company staff, and other key figures, to openly discuss and recognize potential risks. This method is particularly useful as it allows for a diversified view of risks due to the variety of perspectives involved.

- **Documentation:**
  Thorough analysis of documentation represents another crucial step in risk identification. This involves examining previous reports, past incidents, and similar cases to identify trends and potential risks. Past mistakes often provide valuable lessons on how to avoid or mitigate similar risks in the future.

- **Process analysis:**

  A critical inspection of business and IT processes is a highly effective practice to identify potential weaknesses or vulnerabilities. Through this methodology, anomalies or inefficiencies that could pose risks to the organization can be discovered.

- **Interviews:**

  Conducting interviews with key personnel, stakeholders, and other relevant actors provides a deeper and more detailed understanding of potential risks. These conversations can bring to light unknown or overlooked aspects and offer a human perspective on risks.

- **Threat assessment:**

  This phase involves a thorough examination of common threats such as malware, hacking, human errors, natural disasters, and more. The goal is to assess how these threats might affect the organization, considering both the likelihood and the magnitude of the impact.

- **Hypothetical scenarios:**

  Creating hypothetical scenarios is a strategy that allows for simulating specific events and assessing how they might affect the organization's IT environment. This approach helps identify unexpected or less obvious risks.

Once risks have been identified through these methodologies, it is crucial to document them accurately and comprehensively. This documentation should include a detailed description of each risk, assessments of the likelihood of occurrence, as well as an evaluation of its potential impact on the organization. This information will be essential to inform the subsequent phases of the IT risk management process, enabling the organization to develop appropriate mitigation strategies and contingency plans to proactively address these threats.

Risk assessment

Risk assessment is the next phase after identification. This process involves evaluating the severity and probability of previously identified risks to determine which ones require prioritized management.

Risk assessment techniques include:

- **Qualitative assessment:**
  Involves assessing risks based on qualitative factors, such as the severity of impact and the likelihood of occurrence. Risks are classified using descriptive

categories, such as "low," "medium," or "high." This method provides an overview of risks, allowing businesses to identify areas of greater concern without delving into complex numerical details. However, qualitative assessment may lack precision in terms of quantitative data.

- **Quantitative assessment:**
  Uses numerical data to assign a value to risks, allowing for a more detailed analysis of potential costs and benefits associated with risk management. Quantitative assessment involves calculations based on probability and financial impact, providing a more accurate estimate of possible damages or financial losses. This method is particularly useful when companies want to directly compare risks in terms of monetary value.

- **Risk matrix:**
  Is a visual tool representing the probability and severity of risks in a two-dimensional chart. This visual representation greatly simplifies the identification of prioritized risks, as it allows for quickly pinpointing those with a high impact and high probability. The risk matrix is a valuable communication tool that can be used to engage

stakeholders in understanding risks.

- **Criticality analysis:**
  Considers the degree of criticality of a risk by evaluating its effect on the business objective or operational continuity. In other words, not all risks are equal, and criticality analysis helps identify those that might have the greatest impact on the organization's success. This method is particularly useful for focusing attention on threats that could have serious or irreversible consequences.

Risk classification

After assessing the risks, it is important to classify them into categories or levels of priority to focus risk management resources on the most relevant threats. This process ensures that the organization utilizes its resources efficiently and effectively, addressing the most pressing challenges.

Below, we will delve into the common categories of risk classification in detail:

- **Strategic risks:**
  Concern the strategic direction of the organization. They include:

- Threats related to changes in the market,

- Emergence of new competitors

- Technological developments that could challenge the company's competitive position.

Managing strategic risks requires careful long-term planning and adaptation to the changing dynamics of the market.

- **Operational risks:**

Closely linked to the organization's day-to-day operations.

Operational risks can stem from:

- Human errors,

- Service interruptions,

- Technical failures,

- Cybersecurity breaches.

Managing operational risks is crucial to ensuring operational continuity and the quality of services offered.

- **Financial risks:**

This category pertains to financial issues and may include:

- Fluctuations in exchange rates,

- Regulatory changes affecting financial aspects of the company,

- Issues with financial investments.

Managing financial risks is fundamental to protecting the organization's financial assets.

- **Compliance risks:**

  Associated with non-compliance with regulations and regulations, which can lead to legal sanctions, fines, or even compromise the company's image. Managing compliance risks requires strict adherence to relevant laws and regulations, along with rigorous internal oversight and control.

- **Reputational risks:**

  Concern the loss of the organization's reputation. Reputation is an asset and can be damaged by scandals, violations of customer privacy, or poor crisis management. Managing reputational risks is essential to preserving public trust and the company's credibility.

Risk classification provides a clear framework for organizing and prioritizing mitigation activities. This process enables companies to focus on risk categories that can have the most significant impact on operations and business objectives.

The choice of risk classification categories will depend on the specificity of the organization, its industry, and its operational context.

Risk Assessment Methodologies

Risk assessment is a crucial step in IT risk management, and assessment methodologies, including qualitative and quantitative analysis, the use of risk matrices, and result evaluation, help identify, assess, and address risks effectively. The choice of methodologies depends on the specific needs of the organization and the complexity of the risks faced.

Use of risk matrices

Risk matrices are visual tools used in risk assessment to represent the probability and severity of risks in a tabular format. These matrices allow for a quick visualization of risks and identification of prioritized ones.

A typical risk matrix has two axes:

- **Probability Axis:**
  Represents the likelihood of the risk occurring, often divided into categories such as "low," "medium," and "high."

- **Consequence Axis:**
  Represents the severity of the impact of the risk, also divided into categories such as "low," "medium," and "high."

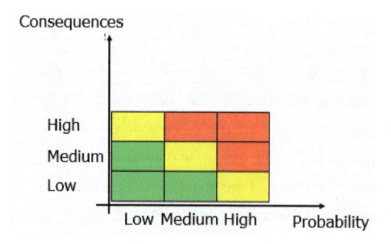

Risks are then positioned on the matrix based on their probabilities and consequences, allowing for the visual identification of those in the high-risk zone that require immediate attention.

Evaluation of risk assessment results

The evaluation of results is the bridge that connects risk identification to practical management.

This phase ensures that risks are adequately understood, prioritized, and addressed efficiently. The ability to interpret and act based on risk assessment results is crucial for the organization's security, operational continuity, and its ability to adapt to changing market and IT conditions.

The evaluation of results may include:

- **Risk prioritization:**
  Once risks are identified and assessed, it is necessary to classify them based on their severity and probability. This process helps pinpoint risks that require immediate interventions. Risks with a high impact and significant probability should receive the utmost attention, while those with a lower impact or probability may be addressed with less urgency.

- **Definition of mitigation strategies:**
  Based on the risk assessment, it is essential to develop specific strategies to mitigate or manage identified risks. These strategies may include the implementation of preventive measures, emergency plans, crisis management procedures, or changes in operational practices. Strategies should be aimed at reducing the potential impact of risks and preventing their occurrence.

- **Resource allocation:**
  Effective allocation of resources is vital to ensure that mitigation actions are successfully implemented. Financial, human, and technical resources should be assigned based on the priority of risks. This means that high-priority risks will receive more significant resources and greater attention from the organization.

- **Communication of results:**
  Transparency and communication are crucial for engaging all stakeholders. The results of the risk assessment should be communicated clearly and comprehensively to all levels of the organization, as well as external stakeholders if applicable. This ensures a common understanding of risks and the

actions needed to address them.

- **Continuous monitoring:**

  Risk assessment is an evolving process. Constantly monitoring risks and updating the assessment based on changes in the business or IT environment is essential. Business and technological environments are in constant flux, and risks may emerge or evolve over time. Continuous monitoring enables readiness to adapt to new challenges.

Threat and Vulnerability Management

Threat and vulnerability management is a continuous and dynamic process that requires ongoing commitment from the organization.

Identifying threats, pinpointing vulnerabilities, and effectively mitigating them are crucial steps to ensure cybersecurity and protect sensitive organizational data.

Identification of Cyber Threats

The identification of cyber threats represents one of the

foundational steps in IT risk management, as it helps identify potential hazards that could jeopardize the security of an organization's IT environment. This process involves considering a wide range of threat sources, ranging from external attackers to malicious insiders and even natural events.

To identify these threats, it is essential to adopt a comprehensive approach that includes:

- **Environmental Analysis:**
  A thorough understanding of the IT environment is a crucial prerequisite for threat identification. This process begins with mapping networks, applications, and sensitive data. Additionally, it is important to identify critical points and interconnections between various components of the IT infrastructure. This analysis provides a clear view of the entire threat landscape.

- **Threat Intelligence:**
  Continuous monitoring of the threat landscape is essential for detecting emerging threats. This can be achieved through consulting threat intelligence feeds that provide up-to-date information on new malware, vulnerabilities, and attacker tactics. Furthermore, analyzing past incidents and involving

security experts can help identify specific threats and their attack methodologies.

- **Threat Assessment:**
  Once threats are identified, it is important to classify them based on the likelihood of occurrence and potential impact. This threat assessment helps determine which threats require immediate attention and which can be addressed with a less urgent management approach. Classifying threats allows for the focus of resources on managing the most relevant and dangerous threats.

- **Threat Modeling:**
  Creating threat models is a key step in defense planning. These models represent typical and possible attack scenarios. For example, they might include phishing attacks, data breaches, or specific vulnerability exploits. Building threat models enables companies to prepare specifically to face these threats by developing targeted security measures and response plans.

Identification of Vulnerabilities

Once vulnerabilities are identified, corrective measures can be implemented, such as security patches, stricter corporate policies, or improvements in operational processes, to reduce the risk of successful attacks. However, it is important to emphasize that vulnerability identification is an ongoing process, as new vulnerabilities may emerge over time or due to changes in the IT environment. Therefore, IT risk management requires constant vigilance and the adoption of proactive security practices.

Identification of vulnerabilities may include:

- **Vulnerability Scanning and Assessment:**
  A common approach to identify vulnerabilities is the use of scanning and analysis tools. These tools can examine source code of applications, network configurations, and weaknesses in operating systems. Vulnerability scanning can reveal issues such as security flaws in code, insecure network configurations, or missing security patches. Vulnerability assessment helps determine the severity and priority of each identified vulnerability.

- **Review of Business Processes:**
  Vulnerabilities are not limited to technical aspects alone. Business processes can also have vulnerabilities, often related to procedures or

operational practices. Reviewing business processes helps identify potential issues related to unauthorized access, credential management, insufficient staff training, or outdated procedures. Process review is crucial as these vulnerabilities can be exploited by both malicious insiders and external attackers.

- **Penetration Testing:**
  Simulated penetration tests are an advanced method to identify vulnerabilities in a controlled environment. These tests mimic real attacks, allowing security experts to assess the actual resilience of the system. During penetration tests, experts attempt to exploit known vulnerabilities or those discovered during the test to demonstrate how an attacker could penetrate the system. These tests are useful for identifying weaknesses that may not emerge through other forms of assessment.

Mitigating Threats and Vulnerabilities

Cybersecurity is an ongoing process that requires constant attention, regular updates, and a continuous commitment to keeping pace with the evolving landscape of cyber threats. In this way, companies can significantly reduce the risk of breaches and effectively protect their data and systems.

Mitigation strategies should be based on a layered approach involving:

- **Technical Protection:**
  Technical protection is the first layer of defense and involves the implementation of technical measures. These may include firewalls, intrusion detection systems (IDS), antivirus systems, and regular software updates. Firewalls filter unwanted network traffic and block potential threats. IDS constantly monitor the environment for suspicious activity and report any intrusions. Antivirus programs detect and remove malware, while software updates fix known vulnerabilities.

- **Policies and Procedures:**
  Defining clear policies and procedures is crucial for good cybersecurity hygiene. These policies should cover aspects such as access controls, strong passwords, patch management, and the sharing of sensitive information. Ensuring that all employees are aware of and adhere to these policies is crucial

for ensuring consistency in cybersecurity.

- **Awareness and Training:**
  The human aspect of cybersecurity is often the weak point. Users may be exposed to threats through unaware or careless actions. Therefore, it is essential to educate staff on cybersecurity, raising awareness about common threats and safe behaviors. Education can cover threat identification, handling suspicious emails, safe browsing practices, and more.

- **Incident Response Planning:**
  While preventive measures are fundamental, it is equally important to prepare for a potential breach or incident. A detailed incident response plan provides instructions on how to manage and contain a threat when it occurs. This includes identifying, isolating, and responding to threats, as well as communicating with stakeholders and resuming normal operations.

- **Continuous Monitoring and Updates**
  Cybersecurity is an ever-evolving process as threats and vulnerabilities constantly change. Implementing a continuous monitoring process for the IT environment is essential to promptly detect and

respond to emerging threats and new vulnerabilities. This process may involve the use of monitoring tools, event logging, network traffic analysis, and verification of security patches.

Compliance and Regulations

Businesses must understand relevant regulations and standards, implement appropriate security measures, and continually monitor compliance to avoid legal implications and sanctions.

Compliance is not only a legal responsibility but also a fundamental part of effective IT risk management to safeguard the organization's data and reputation.

Regulations and Standards

Regulations and standards provide essential guidance for businesses in the realm of information security and IT risk management. Following such standards not only helps ensure legal compliance but also represents good security practice. Moreover, many standards and regulations incorporate risk management principles, assisting businesses in identifying, assessing, and mitigating threats and vulnerabilities consistently and strategically.

Some of the most relevant standards and regulations include:

- **ISO 27001:**
  ISO 27001 is one of the primary international standards for information security management. It provides a comprehensive framework for establishing, implementing, managing, and improving an Information Security Management System (ISMS). This standard helps businesses systematically identify and address IT risks, ensuring the protection of business information and customer-sensitive data.

- **GDPR (General Data Protection Regulation):**
  GDPR is a European regulation that establishes stringent rules for protecting personal data of European Union citizens. Companies must comply with GDPR provisions when handling personal data. This regulation includes obligations related to data breach notification, consent of data subjects, and the appointment of a Data Protection Officer.

- **HIPAA (Health Insurance Portability and Accountability Act):**
  HIPAA is a specific standard for the healthcare industry in the United States. It defines rules for protecting patients' health data and sets strict requirements for the privacy and security of medical data. Healthcare companies must ensure the confidentiality and integrity of patient data.

- **PCI DSS (Payment Card Industry Data Security Standard):**
  PCI DSS is aimed at businesses handling payment card data. This standard defines specific requirements to protect this sensitive information. Companies processing credit card payments must comply with PCI DSS to ensure the security of customers' financial data.

- **NIST Cybersecurity Framework:**
  States, the NIST Cybersecurity Framework provides guidelines to enhance an organization's cybersecurity. It is based on five key principles: identify, protect, detect, respond, and recover. This framework helps businesses assess their cybersecurity and develop plans to mitigate risks.

Compliance with IT Regulations

Compliance with IT regulations not only reduces the risk of penalties and fines but also contributes to building a reputation of reliability and security. It further helps protect sensitive customer and user data, reducing the risk of privacy breaches.

Effective compliance management requires continuous commitment, dedicated resources, and constant updates to policies and security measures to adapt to changing cyber threats and regulatory changes.

Companies should adopt the following practices to ensure compliance:

- **Assessment of Compliance:**
  The first step to ensure compliance is to identify which IT regulations apply to the organization. This

can vary depending on the industry, geographical location, and the type of data processed. Understanding the specific requirements of each regulation is crucial, as they can vary significantly. ***E.g.:*** *the General Data Protection Regulation (GDPR) focuses on protecting personal data, while PCI DSS concerns the security of payment card information.*

- **Implementation of Security Measures:**
  Once compliance requirements are identified, the organization must adopt necessary security measures and procedures to meet those requirements. These measures can vary significantly and may include data encryption, permission management, activity logging, physical protection of resources, access control, and many other aspects. Implementing such measures may require significant investments in technology, training, and human resources.

- **Continuous Monitoring:**
  Compliance is not a one-time effort but a continuous process. Companies should conduct constant monitoring to ensure that policies and security measures are maintained and adhered to over time. This involves monitoring systems for policy violations

or breaches, ensuring employees follow security procedures, and updating security measures in response to new risks or regulatory requirements.

- **Reporting and Documentation:**
  Documentation is an essential element to demonstrate compliance to regulatory bodies. Companies should maintain an accurate record of actions taken to maintain compliance. This could include logging changes made to systems, procedures followed to ensure data security, and measures taken to respond to security incidents. Additionally, periodic reports should be prepared to demonstrate compliance to regulatory bodies or internal auditors.

Legal Implications and Sanctions

It is crucial to emphasize that legal implications and sanctions can vary significantly depending on the country, region, and type of regulation violated. Therefore, it is essential for companies to fully understand the IT laws and regulations that apply to them and take proactive measures to ensure compliance.

This may include adopting security policies, implementing

adequate technical measures, and providing staff training to reduce the risk of breaches and legal consequences.

Effective IT risk management is crucial to avoid severe legal consequences and protect both the organization and customer data.

Some potential consequences may include:

- **Economic Sanctions:**

  Economic sanctions can be among the most immediate and burdensome consequences for companies that violate IT regulations. Regulatory authorities, such as the Data Protection Authority (under GDPR), have the power to impose significant fines. Sanctions can vary widely based on the severity of the violation and the specific regulation but can reach substantial amounts. Fines serve both as a penalty for non-compliance and as a deterrent to encourage rule compliance.

- **Legal Actions:**

  Companies that fail to comply with data protection laws or other IT regulations may be subject to legal actions. Customers or affected individuals can take legal action to seek compensation for damages suffered due to data security breaches. These legal actions can result in significant costs for legal defense and compensation payments.

- **Reputational Damage:**
Cybersecurity breaches can severely damage the organization's reputation. The loss of sensitive data or breaches of customer privacy can lead to a loss of trust from customers, business partners, and the public. This loss of trust can translate into customer losses, reduced business opportunities, and lasting damage to the company's image.

- **Criminal Sanctions:**
In severe cases of cybersecurity breaches, criminal sanctions may be envisaged. These sanctions can involve legal actions against corporate executives or individuals responsible for cybersecurity who neglected data protection or failed to comply with IT laws and regulations. Criminal sanctions may include personal fines, criminal liability, and even imprisonment, depending on the severity of the violations.

Business Impact Analysis (BIA)

Business Impact Analysis (BIA) is an essential tool for understanding the impact of disruptions to business processes and planning effective IT risk management.

Utilizing BIA results to identify risks, plan for business continuity, and ensure regulatory compliance is crucial for ensuring business resilience and the protection of critical data.

Concept of BIA

Business Impact Analysis is a mandatory step in the context of IT risk management.

This process not only allows companies to identify potential impacts of disruptions to business processes but also plays a key role in providing a detailed view of activities, systems, data, and resources that constitute the core of the organization's operations.

Let's see how its main components contribute to building business resilience:

- **Identification of critical processes:**
  The first phase of BIA involves accurately identifying the business processes that are essential for the organization's operation. These processes can range from the production of goods or services to distribution, human resource management, financial management, and more. Recognizing these critical processes is the first step in the journey toward managing business continuity.

- **Estimation of impacts:**
  Once critical processes are identified, it is crucial to assess the importance of each in terms of potential financial loss, impact on the company's reputation,

legal risks, and the need to remain in compliance with current regulations. This analysis contributes to establishing a priority hierarchy, ensuring that resources are allocated proportionally based on strategic importance.

- **Identification of Recovery Time Objectives (RTO):**
  Defining the maximum time within which each critical process must be restored after an interruption is one of the milestones of BIA. This step determines how long the organization can endure an interruption before significant damage occurs.
  E.g.: *a company might establish that its production process must be restored within 48 hours to avoid severe financial losses.*

- **Identification of the Recovery Point Objective (RPO):**
  Defining the maximum time frame within which the organization aims to restore data after an interruption. The RPO determines how much data the organization can afford to lose in case of an incident before significant impacts occur, emphasizing the importance of planning for the protection and recovery of critical data.

E.g.: *if a company sets an RPO of 2 hours, it means it seeks to restore data up to two hours before the incident, limiting the data loss to this time frame.*

- **Estimation of resource requirements:**
  In addition to establishing recovery times, BIA also involves identifying the resources needed to bring critical processes back to normalcy in the event of an interruption. These resources may include qualified personnel, technology, backup data, alternative workspaces, and more. The precise determination of such requirements is crucial for business continuity planning and resource allocation.

How to Conduct a BIA

Conducting a BIA requires a systematic approach and involves several key phases:

- **Identification of stakeholders:**
  Involving key stakeholders within the organization is the first fundamental step in the BIA process. These stakeholders may include process owners, IT managers, and risk management personnel. Their participation is crucial to ensuring a comprehensive understanding of processes and associated risks.

- **Definition of BIA objectives:**

  Clearly establishing BIA objectives at the beginning of the process is essential. Objectives may vary from assessing the financial impacts of process disruptions to determining recovery requirements for ensuring business continuity. Clearly defining objectives guides the entire BIA process.

- **Data collection:**

  The next phase involves collecting detailed data on business processes. This data should include information on workflow, involved resources, critical data, and recovery objectives. This phase requires an in-depth analysis of business processes, including those supporting essential operations.

- **Impact assessment:**

  Using the data collected in the previous phase, it is possible to proceed with the assessment of the impacts of disruptions to business processes. This assessment should cover various aspects, including financial and operational impacts. Additionally, it should lead to the determination of Recovery Time Objectives (RTOs), defining the maximum acceptable time for process restoration, and resource requirements needed to achieve these objectives.

- **BIA reports:**

  The results of the BIA should be carefully documented in a comprehensive report. This report should include a classification of critical processes based on impact and recovery priorities. This classification will guide the subsequent business continuity-planning phase, allowing the organization to develop targeted mitigation strategies and emergency response plans.

Using BIA Results in Risk Management

The results of the BIA are an important resource to ensure that the organization is prepared to address and mitigate risks related to disruptions in business processes.

Here's how to leverage BIA results for effective IT risk management:

- **Risk identification:**

  One of the primary contributions of BIA is the identification of specific risks that could impact critical business processes. These risks may arise from various sources, including technical failures, human errors, cyber threats, natural disasters, and more. With data collected from BIA, it is possible to make an accurate assessment of specific risks and vulnerabilities that require attention.

- **Business continuity planning:**
Based on the identified Recovery Time Objectives (RTOs) in BIA, detailed business continuity plans can be developed. These plans define the actions needed to restore business processes in the event of an interruption. RTOs indicate the maximum acceptable time for recovery, helping establish priorities and action sequences to ensure business continuity.

- **Resource allocation:**
The resource requirements identified in BIA, such as qualified personnel, technology, alternative workspaces, and backup data, provide guidelines for allocating the resources necessary for business process recovery. This aspect is crucial to ensure that the organization has essential resources for timely process restoration.

- **IT risk management:**
Incorporate BIA results into IT risk assessment and mitigation strategies. Focus on protecting critical business processes and reducing risks that could negatively impact business continuity. Integrating

BIA data into IT risk management helps define priorities and optimize resources to address risks effectively.

- **Regulatory compliance:**
Ensure that business continuity plans developed based on BIA results comply with relevant IT regulations. This may include regulations such as the General Data Protection Regulation (GDPR) or ISO 27001 (information security regulation). Regulatory compliance is essential to avoid sanctions and legal issues associated with data and security management.

Business Continuity Plan (BCP)

Business Continuity Planning (BCP) aims to ensure the operational continuity of the organization in the event of disruptions or IT disasters.

Creation of a Business Continuity Plan

Creating a business continuity plan is a mandatory step in IT risk management and preparing for critical interruptions. This plan is designed to outline actions to be taken in the event of events that could threaten the organization's operations.

Here is a detailed overview of the key steps in creating a BCP:

- **Risk Assessment:**
  The starting point in creating a BCP is risk assessment. This process involves identifying and assessing computer threats and vulnerabilities in the organization's IT environment. This assessment helps understand potential causes of interruptions, enabling a focus on protecting and mitigating specific risks.

- **Identification of Critical Processes:**
  Within the BCP framework, it is essential to identify critical business processes that must be quickly restored to ensure operational continuity. These processes can range from data management and customer communication to the production of goods

or services. Identifying and prioritizing them is a key part of defining the BCP.

- **Impact Analysis:**
  To determine the success of the BCP, a detailed analysis of potential impacts resulting from interruptions of critical processes is necessary. This analysis covers a wide range of impacts, including financial, operational, and reputational. This data helps establish recovery requirements, including Recovery Time Objectives (RTO), defining the maximum acceptable time for recovery.

- **Development of Recovery Plans:**
  BCP requires the definition of detailed procedures for the recovery of IT operations. This includes developing emergency plans, backup procedures, data recovery strategies, and critical process recovery plans. These plans must be comprehensive and specific, indicating who is responsible for what and what actions must be taken in the event of an interruption.

- **Testing and Exercises:**
  An effective BCP must undergo regular testing and exercises. These tests simulate emergency situations and verify whether the plan works in practice.

Additionally, they provide staff with the opportunity to understand how to react in case of interruptions and identify any areas that require improvement.

- **Continuous Updates:**
  The IT environment is constantly evolving, and computer threats change over time. Therefore, it is crucial to keep the BCP updated to reflect changes in technology, organization, and computer threats. Continuous updating ensures that the plan remains relevant and ready to face new challenges.

Restoration of IT Operations

Restoration of IT operations is a critical component of BCP as IT increasingly becomes the primary component of modern business operations.

Some key aspects of IT operations restoration include:

- **Identification of Priorities:**
  The first step in restoring IT operations is identifying priorities. It is crucial to determine which IT systems and services must be restored immediately to ensure operational continuity. This may include key servers supporting critical applications, essential network connectivity for communications, or e-commerce

services generating revenue. Identifying these priorities guides the restoration sequence and resource allocation.

- **Backup and Data Restoration:**
Data protection is of primary importance. A robust backup system must be implemented to ensure that critical data is copied and securely stored. In the event of an interruption, data restoration must be a priority. This involves creating regular backup copies, verifying data integrity, and readiness for quick restoration. Encryption and secure access policies are also essential to protect sensitive data.

- **Recovery Infrastructure:**
Maintaining adequate recovery infrastructure is essential to ensure operational continuity. This infrastructure may include geographically separated recovery sites, backup servers, and virtualization systems. Virtualization allows for quickly launching applications on backup servers or virtual machines, reducing downtime. The recovery infrastructure should be ready for use and periodically tested to verify its effectiveness.

- **Trained Personnel:**
An IT recovery plan is effective only if the staff is

prepared to execute necessary procedures in emergency situations. Staff should be trained on recovery procedures, have access to support resources, and understand their roles during operations restoration. Regular training and skill updates are essential to ensure that staff is ready to respond effectively.

Example of a BCP

Here is a simplified example of how a business continuity plan for managing IT risks might look:

- **BCP Objective:**
  Ensure the operational continuity of the organization in the event of IT disruptions, minimizing financial and operational impacts.

- **Threat Identification:**
  Identify and assess IT threats that could jeopardize business operations. Some identified threats include Distributed Denial of Service (DDoS) attacks, ransomware, and hardware failures.

- **Critical Processes:**
  Identify critical business processes that require special attention and must be quickly restored to

ensure operational continuity.

Critical business processes include:

- **Human Resources Management:**
  Ensure the management of personnel and human resources to avoid disruptions in daily operations.

- **Financial Operations Continuity:**
  Ensure that financial transactions can proceed smoothly to avoid significant financial losses.

- **Customer Data Access:**
  Ensure access to customer data, essential for maintaining business relationships and meeting customer needs.

Impact Analysis:

Evaluate potential financial and operational impacts of interruptions. This analysis helps understand the consequences of interruptions, including daily revenue loss and damage to the company's reputation.

Recovery Plans:

- **Daily Backup of Critical Data:**
  Perform daily backups of critical data and securely archive them to ensure data availability in case of loss or damage.

- **Hot Standby Servers at a Contingency Site:**
  Maintain hot standby servers at a geographically separate contingency site so that operations can be quickly shifted in case of disruptions at the main site.

- **Periodic Staff Training:**
  Ensure that staff is trained in managing interruptions and understands their role during operations restoration.

- **Plan Testing:**
  Conduct quarterly exercises to test the effectiveness of the business continuity plan. These tests include data and IT operations recovery and help identify any areas that require improvement in the plan.

This is just an example of how a business continuity plan might be structured. Each company should tailor its BCP to its needs and the specific IT threats it faces.

Disaster Recovery Plan (DRP)

The Disaster Recovery Plan (DRP) focuses on restoring IT systems and data in the event of disasters or significant disruptions.

Concept of DRP

The Disaster Recovery Plan (DRP) is a strategic plan that outlines how an organization can recover its IT operations after a disaster or an event causing a severe disruption.

These events may include natural disasters, cyber-attacks, hardware failures, or any situation jeopardizing operational continuity. The DRP aims to minimize downtime, reduce financial losses, and safeguard data integrity.

An effective DRP should include:

- **Inventory of Critical IT Systems, Data, and Resources:**

  This inventory provides a comprehensive overview of the organization's IT ecosystem and identifies components vital for operational continuity.

  Here's how to address this aspect in more detail:

  - **Identification of Critical Systems:**

    Collaborate closely with departmental managers to pinpoint IT systems and applications essential for business operations. These systems may include servers, databases, software applications, storage systems, and network devices.

  - **Cataloging Critical Data:**

    Carefully assess the data managed by the organization and identify those of crucial importance.

    This data may encompass financial information, customer data, legal documents, research data, and any other information critical to business functioning.

- **Mapping of Resources:**
  Create a comprehensive map of IT resources, including hardware, software, networks, and cloud services. This may involve specifying server configurations, network setups, and utilized cloud infrastructures.

- **Evaluation of Interdependence:**
  Recognize interdependencies among various critical systems and data. This is crucial to understanding how a disruption in one area may impact other parts of the IT system.

- **Detailed Documentation:**
  Maintain detailed documents of the inventory for easy accessibility in emergencies. This documentation should include information on software versions, licenses, authorized users, and backup procedures.

- **Detailed Procedures for System and Data Recovery:**
  These are crucial to ensuring that the organization can efficiently recover after a disaster or interruption. These procedures should be well-structured and easy to follow.

- **Definition of Restoration Processes:**
  For each critical system and data, develop detailed procedures that define how to restore them. These procedures should include specific steps, including commands, scripts, or manual actions necessary for restoration.

- **Prioritization of Recovery Tasks:**
  Establish a restoration sequence based on the importance and dependence of systems. Critical systems for operational continuity should be restored first.

- **Management of Credentials and Authorizations:**
  Ensure that access credentials to systems and data are documented and easily accessible. Ensure that only authorized personnel have access to resources during restoration.

- **Backup and Data Restoration Procedures:** Clearly define how to back up critical data, how to securely archive it, and how to restore it in case of loss. Regularly verify that backups are intact and recoverable.

- **Internal Communication:**

  Define internal communication procedures to inform personnel involved in restoration, including managers, technicians, and system administrators.

- **External Communication:**

  Establish a communication procedure with external stakeholders, such as clients, suppliers, and business partners, to keep them informed of disruptions and progress in the restoration process.

- **Detailed Documentation:**

  Similar to the inventory, it is essential to maintain detailed documentation of restoration procedures so that they are easily accessible and understandable during emergency situations.

- **Communication Procedures to Inform Staff and Stakeholders in Case of Disaster:**

  It is crucial to ensure that staff and stakeholders are informed promptly and clearly in the event of a disaster or interruption

- **Chain of Command:**
  Define a clear chain of command that identifies the individuals responsible for the DRP and their roles in internal and external communication.

- **Communication Planning:**
  Establish protocols for communication, including notification methods, contact lists, and procedures to activate the DRP and alert staff.

- **Continuous Updates:**
  Regularly communicate updates on the restoration status. Provide clear and accurate information on progress and expectations.

- **Staff Involvement:**
  Ensure that staff is adequately trained to understand communication procedures and their responsibilities in case of an emergency.

- **External Communication:**
  Identify external stakeholders, such as clients, suppliers, and regulatory authorities, and establish dedicated communication channels to inform them promptly and accurately.

- **Data Recovery Plan to Ensure Availability of Critical Data:**

  This plan should address the protection, backup, and restoration of critical data. Let's explore how to develop it in more detail:

  - **Data Backup:**

    Define detailed procedures to regularly perform backups of critical data. These backups should be stored in a secure location, ideally offsite, to ensure their availability in case of a disaster.

  - **Data Restoration Testing:**

    Conduct regular data restoration tests to verify the integrity of backups and ensure they can be successfully restored. Document these tests and use them to improve the data restoration process.

  - **Data Protection:**

    Implement security measures to protect critical data from cyber threats such as ransomware or unauthorized access. These measures may include data encryption and access controls.

- **Data Recovery:**
  Establish detailed procedures for data recovery in case of loss or damage. These procedures should include expected recovery times and verification procedures for the integrity of restored data.

- **Process Documentation:**
  Maintain detailed documentation of backup and data restoration procedures so that assigned personnel can effectively follow them in case of an emergency.

- **Periodic Testing to Verify Plan Effectiveness and Implement Improvements:**
  Periodic testing of the Disaster Recovery Plan (DRP) is essential to ensure the plan's effectiveness and identify areas for improvement.
  Here's how to conduct effective tests:

  - **Types of Tests:**
    There are various types of tests, including disaster simulations, data recovery exercises, and verification of restoration procedures. It's crucial to use a variety of approaches to cover all critical areas of the DRP.

- **Testing Frequency:**
  Plan periodic tests, at least annually or whenever significant changes occur in IT systems or procedures. Ensure that the involved personnel are aware of the test dates.

- **Realistic Scenarios:**
  Create realistic test scenarios that mimic potential threats and interruptions that could occur in reality.

- **Results Evaluation:**
  After each test, critically evaluate the results. Identify successes and areas where the plan could be improved.

- **Continuous Improvements:**
  Based on test results, make improvements to the DRP. Document these improvements and incorporate them into the plan itself.

- **Staff Involvement:**
  Involve key personnel in conducting tests and gathering feedback on restoration procedures and communication protocols.

Identification of Critical Systems:

These systems play a fundamental role in the organization's day-to-day operations, and their interruption would have a significant impact.

Here's how to identify critical systems:

- **Analysis of Business Processes:**
  Collaborate with departmental managers to understand which systems and applications are crucial for their operations.

- **Impact Assessment:**
  Evaluate the financial, operational, and reputational impact of an interruption for each critical system. This will help establish priorities in the restoration process.

- **Technological Inventory:**
  Maintain an updated inventory of the hardware and software systems used in the organization, highlighting those deemed critical.

- **Data Assessment:**
  Identify critical data, such as financial information, customer data, legal documents, and intellectual property. Ensure robust backup procedures are in

place for this data.

Recovery Procedures and DRP Testing:

Recovery procedures and testing of the Disaster Recovery Plan (DRP) must ensure that the organization is prepared to successfully handle interruptions to IT systems or disasters. These activities are an essential part of the entire computer risk management process, enabling the DRP to remain effective and adaptable to the organization's continuously evolving needs.

Backup and Restoration of Critical Data:

- **Definition of Backup Processes:**
  Determine which data is critical and establish clear procedures to regularly back up this data. This should include scheduling backup activities, frequency, and storage methods.

- **Security of Backup Data:**
  Ensure that backup data is protected from unauthorized access or cyber threats. Encrypting backup data and storing it in a secure location are good practices.

- **Verification of Backup Data:**

  Regularly verify that backup data is intact and recoverable. Periodically test the restoration of data from backup copies to ensure the process functions as expected.

Restoration of Hardware and Software Systems:

- **Detailed Procedures:**

  For each critical hardware and software system, develop detailed procedures outlining the necessary steps for restoration. These procedures should be clear and understandable so that staff can follow them even in emergency situations.

- **Restoration Prioritization:**

  Establish a priority order for restoring systems. Focus first on fundamental systems and applications for operational continuity.

- **Technical Documentation:**

  Maintain up-to-date technical documentation of hardware and software systems, including details such as configurations, licenses, and dependencies. This documentation is valuable during restoration operations.

Resource Security During Restoration:

- **Access Control:**

  During the restoration process, ensure that only authorized personnel have access to resources. Apply the same security measures that were in place before the interruption.

- **Continuous Monitoring:**

  Constantly monitor the environment during restoration to detect any anomalies or security issues. Security should be a priority even during emergency situations.

Communication with Staff and Stakeholders:

- **Communication Planning:**

  Establish clear protocols for internal and external communication during restoration. Clearly define who is responsible for what in terms of communication.

- **Timely Communication:**

  Inform staff and stakeholders as quickly as possible in case of a disaster or interruption. Provide regular updates on the restoration status and future expectations.

Monitoring Restoration Progress and Evaluating Success:

- **Key Performance Indicators (KPIs):**
  Establish key performance indicators (KPIs) to assess restoration progress, such as expected restoration time compared to actual time. These KPIs can help measure success.

- **Post-Restoration Evaluation:**
  After restoration, conduct a post-mortem evaluation to review the restoration process and identify areas for improvement. This evaluation should contribute to refining the DRP for future emergencies.

Periodic Testing to Verify Plan Effectiveness and Implement Improvements:

- **Testing Frequency:**
  Schedule periodic tests as part of a continuous improvement strategy. The testing frequency should be sufficient to ensure that the DRP remains up-to-date and adaptable to new threats and changes in the IT environment.

- **Realistic Scenarios:**
  Use realistic test scenarios based on potential threats and interruptions that the organization may face in

reality.

- **Feedback and Improvements:**
  After each test, gather feedback from involved
  personnel and use the results to make improvements
  to the DRP. Ensure that corrections are implemented
  effectively.

Security Policy Management

The management of security policies represents a fundamental element within the broader framework of risk management.

Security policies form the foundation upon which the protection of corporate assets, sensitive data, and operational integrity is built.

This chapter will focus on the creation, implementation, and continuous management of security policies within an organization.

Security Policies

The creation and implementation of security policies are crucial phases in mitigating risks and ensuring the organization's security.

During this phase, the primary goal is to develop a set of clear and documented directives outlining the security measures necessary to protect corporate assets and information.

Some key steps in this phase include:

- **Risk and Security Needs Analysis:**
  Before defining security policies, it is essential to conduct a risk analysis.
  This analysis identifies potential threats and vulnerabilities of the organization, allowing for the determination of the most appropriate security measures.
  Security needs vary significantly among companies and should be assessed based on industry, size, managed data, and other factors.

- **Definition of Security Policies:**

  Security policies should be drafted clearly and comprehensibly for all stakeholders. These policies must include guidelines on passwords, resource access, data sharing, device management, physical protection, and more. Additionally, it is important to establish clear responsibilities for policy enforcement.

- **Stakeholder Involvement:**

  Stakeholder involvement is essential to ensure that security policies are supported and implemented throughout the organization. Stakeholders include not only management and the security team but also employees, suppliers, and business partners. Clearly communicating policies and providing security training and awareness are crucial for gaining adherence.

Stakeholder Involvement

Stakeholders encompass all interested parties both within and outside the organization who can influence or be influenced by information security.

This involvement is essential to ensure that security policies are effective and widely accepted.

Some key points to consider include:

- **Internal Involvement:**

  - **Executive Leadership:**
    xecutive leadership must be actively involved in defining and approving security policies. They should advocate for a culture of security throughout the organization.

  - **Employees:**
    End users must be aware of security policies and trained to follow them. Employee involvement is crucial for preventing internal threats.

  - **Security Team:**
    The security team should collaborate with other business functions to ensure that policies align with the operational and technological needs of the organization.

- **External Involvement:**

  - **Suppliers:**
    Security policies should extend to interactions with suppliers and business partners. It should be clear how they are expected to

handle data and comply with organizational policies.

- **Regulatory Authorities:**
  If the organization is subject to specific regulations, involving regulatory authorities is crucial to ensure compliance.

- **Customers and External Users:**
  If customers or external users are concerned about security policies, involving them in the definition and adherence to these policies is necessary.

Monitoring and Review of Policies

Security policies are not static but must undergo continuous monitoring and review to remain effective over time. This critical phase in IT risk management ensures that policies stay relevant, adapt to new threats, and align with technological changes.

Some key aspects to consider in this phase include:

- **Policy Monitoring:**

  - **Use of Tools and Metrics:**
    t is essential to use tools and metrics to monitor compliance with security policies.

These tools may include breach detection systems, access logs, multi-factor authentication systems, and more. Metrics can be used to measure the degree of compliance with policies and identify any non-compliance areas.

- **Regular Threat and Vulnerability Assessments:**

  The landscape of cybersecurity threats is constantly evolving. Therefore, conducting regular assessments of threats and vulnerabilities is crucial to adapt security policies accordingly. This assessment may involve analyzing threat trends, consulting vulnerability databases, and participating in threat information sharing communities.

- **Periodic Review:**

  - **Scheduled Review Planning:**

    It is important to schedule periodic reviews of security policies. These reviews should be conducted based on a predetermined calendar and involve a team of IT security experts. The goal is to ensure that policies are up-to-date and remain suitable for current challenges.

- **Stakeholder Involvement:**
  During reviews, involving key stakeholders is crucial. These may include IT staff, security managers, business executives, and employees. Ensure that policies are understood, accepted, and relevant to the entire organization.

- **Updates and Improvements:**

  - **Implementation of Updates and Improvements:**
    Based on the results of monitoring and reviews, it is necessary to implement updates and improvements to security policies. These updates may include new guidelines, operational procedures, security requirements, and technological controls. Changes should address emerging threats and identified vulnerability areas.

  - **Communication of Changes:**
    Any changes made to policies must be communicated clearly to all stakeholders. This ensures that the staff understands the new directives and can adhere to the updated policies.

Incident Response and Management

The management of security incidents is crucial to minimize damages, protect sensitive data, and ensure operational continuity.

It requires careful planning, a swift and effective response, and a detailed post-incident analysis to ensure both cybersecurity and the operational continuity of the organization.

Preparation for Cybersecurity Incidents

This phase involves the development of a robust Incident Response Plan (IRP), which should clearly outline the incident management process, the roles and responsibilities of involved staff, and the necessary resources.

Some key points to consider include:

- **Identification of Threats:**
  Understanding potential threats to the organization is crucial, taking into account current trends in the cybersecurity world. This identification can help establish a solid foundation for incident preparedness.

- **Establishment of an Incident Response Team:**
  The organization should form a team of experts dedicated to incident management. This team should include IT professionals, legal experts, communicators, and representatives from the corporate leadership. Regular training and team preparation are essential for an effective response.

- **Detailed Documentation:**
  Detailed documentation of procedures, protocols, and available resources is crucial. These documents should be readily accessible and regularly updated to ensure that the staff is well-prepared.

- **Incident Simulations:**
  Conducting exercises and incident simulations can

help assess the effectiveness of the incident response plan and identify areas that require improvement.

Incident Response

Once a cybersecurity incident has been verified, a timely and effective response is essential to contain the damage and restore the situation to normalcy.

Some key aspects of an incident response include:

- **Isolation and Containment:**
  Identify the scope of the incident and take measures to contain further damage. This may involve disconnecting compromised systems or isolating infected networks.

- **Communication:**
  Timely communication of the incident to all stakeholders, both internal and external, is crucial. Transparency is essential for managing the perception and trust of the organization.

- **Investigation and Mitigation:**
  Conduct a detailed investigation to determine the origin and nature of the incident. Based on this information, take mitigation measures such as

removing malware, addressing vulnerabilities, and restoring services.

Post-Incident Analysis and Continuous Improvement

After successfully managing the incident, conducting a thorough post-incident analysis is crucial to draw valuable insights and enhance preparedness for the future.

This phase includes:

- **Performance Evaluation:**
  Examine the effectiveness of the incident response, identifying what was successfully managed and areas that require improvement.

- **IRP Update:**
  Use of the information gathered during the post-incident analysis to update the Incident Response Plan (IRP), including processes, roles, and procedures. This is a critical step to ensure that the organization is better prepared for future incidents.

- **Training and Awareness:**
  Building on the post-incident analysis, reinforce staff training and cybersecurity awareness to prevent

future incidents.

- **Legal Compliance and Reporting:**
Ensure compliance with all legal obligations related to the incident, such as notifying data breaches to the relevant authorities or affected parties.

Vendor and Third-Party Management

Companies often rely on a complex network of external partners to provide services, products, or resources that contribute to operational success.

However, with this dependency, potential risks arise that must be adequately addressed to ensure the security and operational continuity of the company.

Risks Associated with External Vendors

The risks associated with external vendors are diverse and can vary significantly depending on the industry and the type of services or products provided.

Some common risks associated with external vendors include:

- **Data Security Breaches:**
  Vendors may have access to sensitive or critical organizational data, making them vulnerable to data breaches or information theft.

- **Service Disruptions:**
  Dependency on vendors for key services could result in unforeseen service disruptions, affecting the operational continuity of the organization.

- **Quality or Compliance Issues:**
  Vendors may fail to meet quality standards or regulations, leading to non-compliant products or services.

- **Financial Issues:**
  The financial stability of vendors can impact the organization's stability, especially if vendors face

financial difficulties or go bankrupt.

- **Corporate Reputation:**
  Actions or scandals involving vendors can damage the organization's reputation, particularly if the organization is associated with the vendors' misconduct.

Vendor Security Assessment

Assessing the security of vendors is a critical step in managing risks associated with third parties.

This assessment should include:

- **Risk Analysis:**
  Determine the level of risk associated with each vendor based on the type of service or product provided, the degree of access to data or systems, and other relevant factors.

- **Security Audits:**
  Conduct regular audits to assess the vendor's compliance with regulations and security standards. These audits should be comprehensive and based on measurable metrics.

- **Evaluation of Vendor Risk Management Practices:**
  Examine the vendor's policies and procedures related to data security, risk mitigation measures, and incident responses.

- **Assessment of Vendor Business Resilience:**
  Verify whether the vendor has effective business continuity plans to address emergencies or incidents.

- **Verification of Certifications and Best Practices:**
  Ensure that the vendor has obtained relevant security certifications and follows industry best practices.

Contract and SLA Management

The management of contracts and Service Level Agreements (SLAs) is a cornerstone in third-party and vendor management: it plays a crucial role in ensuring that relationships with external suppliers are transparent, fair, and aligned with the organization's strategic objectives.

This component is not merely a bureaucratic formality but rather a corporate governance strategy that can significantly contribute to risk reduction, performance optimization, and guaranteed operational continuity.

When drafting these contracts, the following objectives should always be kept in mind:

- **Security Requirements:**
  Clearly specify the security requirements that the vendor must adhere to, including access protocols, encryption, identity management, and other security measures.

- **Deadlines and Performance Metrics:**
  Define deadlines and performance metrics within SLAs, allowing the organization to monitor the vendor and ensure that services are delivered appropriately.

- **Audit Rights:**
  Include in the contract the possibility for the organization to conduct periodic security audits at the vendor's premises to ensure compliance.

- **Resolution Terms and Contingency Plans:**
  Specify contingency plans and dispute resolution mechanisms in case the vendor fails to meet contractual commitments.

Mitigation Techniques and Cybersecurity

In this chapter, we will examine some of the key mitigation techniques and cybersecurity measures, including: encryption, firewalls, access control, network and device security.

Encryption

Encryption is a fundamental cybersecurity technique involving encapsulating data so that it can only be read by those with the correct decryption key.

Encryption plays a crucial role in safeguarding sensitive data, especially when transferred over insecure networks or stored on devices susceptible to theft or loss.

Relevant aspects of encryption include:

- **Symmetric and Asymmetric Key Encryption:**
  Symmetric key encryption uses a single key for both encrypting and decrypting data, while asymmetric key encryption utilizes a key pair – a public key and a private key. Asymmetric encryption is often employed for secure key exchange.

- **Applications of Encryption:**
  Encryption is applied in various contexts, such as securing internet communications (SSL/TLS), encrypting data on mobile devices, and protecting stored data.

- **Key Management:**
  Key management is a critical aspect of encryption. Keys must be securely handled, regularly renewed, and revoked as necessary to prevent unauthorized access.

- **Legal Compliance:**
  Encryption is often required for compliance with data

protection regulations and laws, such as GDPR in Europe or HIPAA in the United States.

Firewall and Access Control

The effective implementation of firewall and access control techniques serves as a crucial bulwark in defending networks and systems from unauthorized access and external threats.

Let's delve further into the relevant aspects of these security practices:

- **Firewall:**

  Firewalls, whether in the form of hardware devices or software, constitute the first line of defense against potential threats. These virtual guardians filter network traffic based on predefined rules that can be customized to suit the specific needs of an organization.

  Their primary function is to block unauthorized traffic, thus safeguarding networks from intrusions, malware attacks, and other forms of security breaches. Strategically configured, firewalls act as sentinels along the digital perimeter, ensuring a secure and protected online environment.

- **Access Control:**

  Access control is the helm through which user permissions to access specific resources or systems are managed. This process includes several key elements, including authentication, authorization, and password management. Authentication ensures the user's identity, authorization determines access privileges based on assigned roles, while password management ensures that credentials are robust and regularly updated. Introducing a well-structured access control system not only protects sensitive information but also limits the risk of internal abuses, maintaining a secure and controlled digital work environment.

- **Security Policies:**

  Security policies form the foundation on which rules and procedures for both firewalls and access control are based. They define who has access to which resources and how, constituting an indispensable framework for cybersecurity management. Policies provide clear guidance on configuring firewall devices and establish protocols for managing user access. Thoughtful implementation of security policies not only protects against external threats but also creates a cohesive and regulatory-compliant environment.

- **Monitoring and Auditing:**
  Continuous monitoring of network activities and accesses is a crucial element for promptly detecting suspicious behaviors and security breaches. Through advanced tools, it is possible to trace and analyze user activities, identifying potential weaknesses in the system. Periodic audits assess the effectiveness of security policies, ensuring they align with evolving cyber threats and technological developments.

Network and Device Security

Network and device security is a continuum of integrated defenses that requires constant attention and proactive actions.

Only by adopting a holistic approach and implementing these practices synergistically can one build a digital infrastructure that withstands the ever-growing challenges of the cybersecurity landscape.

Let's delve into the key elements that contribute to creating a reliable defense against digital threats:

- **Network Protection:**

  Network security goes beyond simply connecting devices and extends to safeguarding fundamental elements such as routers, switches, and access points from unauthorized access or intrusions. Accurate configuration of network devices is crucial to limit unwanted access and prevent intrusion attempts. The implementation of advanced security protocols, such as Virtual Private Networks (VPN) and encryption of data in transit, constitutes an effective barrier against emerging threats.

- **Endpoint Security:**

  Endpoint security is the virtual armor that protects terminal devices, such as computers, smartphones, and tablets, from a wide spectrum of threats. Malware, ransomware, spyware, and phishing attacks are just a few challenges that require a robust defense. Endpoint security solutions encompass antivirus, antimalware, and personal firewalls, working in synergy to detect and neutralize any threat before it can compromise the integrity of the devices. This proactive approach is essential to maintaining a secure digital environment in a constantly evolving technological world.

- **Updates and Patches:**

  Keeping both devices and network components up to date is imperative to eliminate known vulnerabilities and mitigate security risks. Regular updates, including security patches and operating system updates, serve as a drawbridge to closing potential gaps that attackers might exploit. A well-orchestrated update management process is a proactive strategy to ensure that security is always one step ahead of evolving digital threats.

- **Device Usage Policies:**

  Clearly defining and consistently enforcing device usage policies is another fundamental pillar. These policies outline the rules and procedures that users must follow to ensure secure behavior. This includes the adoption of strong passwords, permission management, and ongoing cybersecurity education. Creating an environment where usage policies are respected becomes crucial to mitigating the risk of negligent or unaware user behavior.

Data Security and Privacy

Data security and privacy are two interconnected pillars that play an increasingly critical role in the Risk Management landscape, especially in a digital era that presents organizations with ever-more sophisticated challenges.

Let's deep dive into the crucial role that the proper management of these aspects plays in building trust, mitigating legal risks, and preserving corporate reputation.

Protection of Sensitive Data

Proper protection of sensitive data is essential to ensure the integrity, confidentiality, and availability of business information. The fundamental starting point is the classification of data based on its sensitivity, enabling the application of security measures proportional to the associated risk, ensuring that resources are directed effectively towards the most critical and vulnerable aspects of the organization's information assets.

Limiting access to sensitive data to authorized individuals or roles is an essential tactic. The use of two-factor authentication and role-based controls creates a robust security perimeter, minimizing the risk of unauthorized access. Encryption emerges as a powerful weapon, ensuring that sensitive data is protected both during transmission and storage, providing a virtual shield against potential malicious interceptions.

Continuous monitoring and regular audits are the digital sentinels that guard the integrity of data. Implementing advanced monitoring systems allows for the detection of suspicious activities or unauthorized access, enabling a timely response to potential threats.

Periodic audits not only ensure compliance with security policies but also provide an opportunity for continuous improvement, adapting security measures based on the evolution of threats and technologies.

Customer Privacy and Personal Data Management

Advanced customer privacy and personal data management go beyond mere compliance, representing an ethical commitment to safeguarding user rights and building a secure and trustworthy digital environment.

Some key aspects include:

- **Regulatory Compliance:**
  It is a non-negotiable starting point: ensuring that an organization complies with data privacy laws and regulations, such as GDPR in Europe or CCPA in California, is crucial to avoid legal sanctions and build a reputation of reliability.
  A proactive approach to regulatory compliance not only ensures the protection of user rights but also lays the foundation for ethical and responsible personal data management.

- **Consent and Transparency:**

  The collection of explicit consents for the management and use of personal data is an ethical cornerstone.

  Providing clear information about the purposes of data processing is equally crucial. This approach not only meets regulatory requirements but also contributes to building a trusting relationship with customers. Transparency is the currency of trust: customers appreciate being informed about how their data is handled and for what purposes it is used.

- **Data Subject Rights:**

  Respecting the rights of data subjects is a crucial commitment. Ensuring the right to access, rectify, and delete personal data is an integral part of responsible privacy management.

  Allowing users to exercise control over their data is not only a regulatory requirement but also demonstrates a tangible commitment to privacy protection and ethical management of personal information.

- **Customer Data Protection:**

  The implementation of appropriate security

measures is essential to protect customer personal data from unauthorized access or breaches. This goes beyond mere regulatory compliance, constituting an active commitment to preserving the integrity and confidentiality of information. Advanced encryption, rigorous access controls, and continuous monitoring are key elements to erect a digital bulwark against increasingly sophisticated threats.

- **Privacy by Design:**

  The "*Privacy by Design*" approach represents a step forward, integrating privacy into the design of systems and business processes.

  This not only reduces the risks of privacy breaches but also demonstrates an intrinsic commitment to data protection. Integrating privacy from the early stages of the data lifecycle highlights the awareness and ethical attention that the organization dedicates to the management of personal information.

Risks Associated with Privacy Violation

Managing risks related to privacy violation requires a combination of policies, technologies, and staff training to effectively mitigate risks and protect personal data.

Among the most significant risks for businesses are:

- **Legal Risks and Sanctions:**
  Companies may face legal sanctions and significant fines if they fail to comply with data privacy laws.

- **Reputation Damage:**
  Privacy breaches can harm the organization's reputation and undermine customer trust.

- **Customer Loss:**
  Privacy violations can lead to significant customer losses, especially if customer personal data is compromised.

- **Financial Risks:**
  Privacy breaches can incur high costs associated with investigation, notification, mitigation, and legal actions.

- **Loss of Intellectual Property:**
  Sensitive information and trade secrets can be compromised in the event of a privacy violation.

Continuous Evaluation and Monitoring

This aspect of the process ensures that an organization can consistently and dynamically identify, assess, and mitigate risks.

The use of security metrics, auditing, and penetration testing, along with continuous monitoring of systems and networks, contributes to ensuring a safer and more resilient environment against security threats.

Security metrics

The risk assessment in a Risk Management system begins with the collection and analysis of security metrics. These metrics provide a framework for understanding the organization's performance and vulnerabilities in relation to security.

Some examples of security metrics include:

- **Detected Vulnerabilities:**
  This metric tracks the number of detected system vulnerabilities and classifies them by severity. Monitoring these vulnerabilities is essential for identifying areas at risk and implementing preventive measures.

- **Average Time for Discovery and Resolution of Vulnerabilities:**
  This metric measures the efficiency of the security team in identifying and resolving vulnerabilities. A short time between discovery and resolution indicates a high level of preparedness and a quick response to threats.

- **Malware Infection Rates:**
  This metric measures how frequently systems are infected with malware. Monitoring infection rates helps understand the level of exposure to cybersecurity threats.

- **Successful Attacks:**

  This metric considers the number of attacks that successfully penetrated the system. Its assessment helps measure the effectiveness of implemented security measures.

Auditing and Penetration Testing

Audits and penetration tests can be conducted internally or externally, but their main objective is to identify vulnerabilities and weaknesses.

- **Auditing:**

  Audits assess the compliance of systems and security practices with company policies and standards. These audits may examine access, permissions, and system configurations, as well as password management practices and access policies.

- **Penetration Testing:**

  Penetration tests simulate real attacks to identify specific vulnerabilities that could be exploited by attackers. These tests may include vulnerability assessments of web applications, network testing, and social engineering tests.

Both approaches provide valuable information about

security and help identify areas where improvements are needed.

Continuous Monitoring of Systems and Networks

This process involves the ongoing surveillance of systems, networks, and user activities to identify suspicious behavior or unauthorized activities.

Some key elements of continuous monitoring include:

- **Intrusion Detection:**
  This involves the timely identification of unauthorized access attempts or anomalous activities. Intrusion detection tools are used to constantly monitor traffic and identify suspicious behaviors.
- **Network Traffic Analysis:**
  Monitoring network traffic allows the identification of patterns of suspicious activity or malicious traffic. This is particularly important for detecting threats such as malware and DDoS attacks.
- **Event Logging:**
  Recording and archiving security events provide a detailed trace of all activities relevant to security.

These logs are useful for analysis and investigation of any incidents.

Continuous monitoring enables the detection of threats in real-time and allows for a prompt response to mitigate risks.

Best Practices and Future Trends

Let's explore some established strategies for risk management, recognized as best practices in the field of IT Risk Management, and delve into emerging trends in cybersecurity.

Best Practices in IT Risk Management

Effective risk management requires the consolidation of the following processes:

- **Continuous Risk Assessment:**
  Risk assessment should be a continuous and dynamic process. IT environments constantly change, and companies must be ready to adapt to new threats and vulnerabilities. This process should involve the regular identification, analysis, and mitigation of risks.

- **Leadership Involvement:**
  Corporate leadership must be involved in risk management to ensure the commitment and resources needed to protect the organization. Risk awareness should start from the top and flow downward, creating organizational commitment to security.

- **Definition of Policies and Procedures:**
  The definition of clear policies and procedures for IT security is essential. These policies should cover access, data usage, protection of sensitive information, password management, network

security, and other critical areas. Policies must be communicated effectively to all staff and consistently enforced.

- **Training and Awareness:**
  An essential part of IT risk management is preparedness for incident management. Companies must develop incident response plans outlining procedures to follow in the event of breaches or other threats. Timely identification and response to incidents can significantly limit damage.

- **Constant Monitoring and Review:**
  Finally, it is crucial to constantly monitor the IT environment, regularly revisit policies and procedures, and adapt them to new threats. The threat landscape is continually evolving, and organizations must remain agile to address these challenges.

Emerging Trends in Cybersecurity

To stay ahead of evolving threats, it is crucial to consider some of the current trends:

- **Artificial Intelligence and Machine Learning:**
  The use of artificial intelligence and machine learning

to detect and respond to threats is becoming increasingly important. These technologies can identify anomalous behaviors and react in real-time.

- **Cloud Security:**
  With the growing adoption of cloud-based services, securing data and applications hosted in the cloud is a priority. Companies must implement cloud-specific security strategies.

- **IoT Security:**
  As Internet of Things (IoT) devices proliferate, the security of these devices has become a critical concern. Managing vulnerabilities in IoT networks is an area of growing importance.

Planning for the Future

In the ever-evolving world of cybersecurity, it is essential not only to address current challenges but also to prepare for emerging long-term risks. Effective future planning is crucial to ensure IT security and operational continuity.

Here are some key aspects:

- **Scenario planning:**
  Companies should conduct scenario exercises to identify potential future risks and develop mitigation

plans. These exercises involve creating hypothetical scenarios that could threaten the organization and assessing response strategies.

For example, a company might examine how it would handle a large-scale cyberattack or a highly sophisticated data breach. This practice helps prepare the organization for critical situations before they occur.

- **Investments in Emerging Technologies:**
  The technological landscape is continually evolving, and new technologies can bring new security challenges. Companies should closely monitor emerging technologies that could impact IT security. This may include adopting artificial intelligence technologies for threat detection, advanced encryption, or securing Internet of Things (IoT) devices. Investments in solutions that address these challenges are often necessary to ensure long-term security.

- **Collaboration Between Companies:**
  Information sharing and collaboration with other organizations can be valuable in anticipating emerging threats and developing response

strategies. Organizations can benefit from participating in industry working groups, threat-sharing forums, or collaborating with government entities and academic institutions. This collaboration widens the perspective on cybersecurity and provides opportunities to learn from others.

Adopting established best practices is crucial but not sufficient to ensure long-term cybersecurity. Monitoring emerging trends, developing mitigation plans based on future scenarios, and collaborating with other organizations are key elements to protect the organization from ever-evolving threats.

Thoughtful future planning ensures that the organization is ready to face the challenges ahead and maintain a secure IT environment.

www.ingramcontent.com/pod-product-compliance
Lightning Source LLC
LaVergne TN
LVHW052056060326
832903LV00061B/986